50 Autumn Gourmet Dishes

By: Kelly Johnson

Table of Contents

- Pumpkin Ravioli
- Butternut Squash Soup
- Caramelized Onion and Goat Cheese Tart
- Roasted Chestnut Soup
- Maple Glazed Brussels Sprouts
- Apple Cider Glazed Pork
- Roasted Root Vegetables
- Mushroom Risotto with Truffle Oil
- Seared Duck Breast with Fig Sauce
- Chestnut and Cranberry Stuffing
- Butternut Squash and Sage Risotto
- Grilled Lamb Chops with Mint Pesto
- Pear and Blue Cheese Salad
- Beef and Pumpkin Chili
- Roasted Pumpkin Seeds
- Spicy Carrot and Ginger Soup
- Roasted Beet Salad with Goat Cheese
- Braised Short Ribs with Root Vegetables
- Cider-Braised Chicken

- Pumpkin and Ricotta Gnocchi
- Roasted Apple and Squash Soup
- Maple-Glazed Carrots
- Autumn Harvest Salad
- Butternut Squash and Sage Flatbread
- Pecan-Crusted Salmon
- Braised Lamb Shanks with Root Vegetables
- Sweet Potato and Kale Salad
- Spiced Pear Cake
- Roasted Brussels Sprouts with Pancetta
- Cranberry and Orange Glazed Turkey
- Roasted Pumpkin with Parmesan
- Herb-Crusted Pork Tenderloin
- Spicy Apple Chutney
- Baked Acorn Squash with Quinoa
- Pear and Arugula Salad with Walnuts
- Autumn Vegetable Gratin
- Chestnut-Stuffed Chicken
- Roasted Sweet Potato with Cinnamon
- Apple Crisp
- Cinnamon Baked Pears

- Stuffed Acorn Squash
- Wild Mushroom and Spinach Frittata
- Caramelized Apple and Onion Tart
- Pumpkin Spice Cheesecake
- Grilled Squash and Zucchini Salad
- Maple Roasted Sweet Potatoes
- Baked Apple with Cinnamon and Nuts
- Apple and Pork Sausage Stuffing
- Carrot and Sweet Potato Soup
- Spiced Pumpkin Cake with Cream Cheese Frosting

Pumpkin Ravioli

Ingredients:

- 1 package of fresh or frozen ravioli (preferably pumpkin-filled)
- 2 tbsp butter
- 1 tbsp olive oil
- 1/4 cup sage leaves
- 1/4 cup grated Parmesan cheese
- Salt and pepper, to taste

Instructions:

1. Cook the ravioli according to the package instructions.
2. While the ravioli cooks, heat the butter and olive oil in a large skillet over medium heat.
3. Add the sage leaves and cook until crispy, about 2-3 minutes.
4. Drain the ravioli and add them to the skillet with the sage. Toss gently to coat.
5. Season with salt and pepper to taste.
6. Plate the ravioli, sprinkle with Parmesan cheese, and serve immediately.

Butternut Squash Soup

Ingredients:

- 1 medium butternut squash, peeled, seeded, and cubed
- 1 onion, chopped
- 2 cloves garlic, minced
- 1 carrot, chopped
- 4 cups vegetable broth
- 1/2 cup coconut milk or heavy cream
- 1 tsp ground ginger
- 1/2 tsp ground nutmeg
- Salt and pepper, to taste
- Olive oil for sautéing

Instructions:

1. In a large pot, heat olive oil over medium heat. Add the chopped onion and cook until softened, about 5 minutes.
2. Add the garlic, carrot, and butternut squash, and cook for another 5 minutes.
3. Pour in the vegetable broth, bring to a boil, and then reduce the heat to a simmer. Cook until the squash is tender, about 20 minutes.
4. Once the squash is soft, use an immersion blender or regular blender to puree the soup until smooth.
5. Stir in the coconut milk (or cream), ginger, nutmeg, salt, and pepper.
6. Simmer for an additional 5 minutes, then serve hot.

Caramelized Onion and Goat Cheese Tart

Ingredients:

- 1 sheet puff pastry
- 2 large onions, thinly sliced
- 2 tbsp butter
- 1 tbsp olive oil
- 4 oz goat cheese, crumbled
- 1 tbsp fresh thyme leaves
- 1 tbsp balsamic vinegar
- Salt and pepper, to taste

Instructions:

1. Preheat the oven to 400°F (200°C).
2. In a skillet, heat butter and olive oil over medium heat. Add the onions and cook, stirring occasionally, until they are caramelized and golden brown, about 20 minutes.
3. Add balsamic vinegar to the onions and cook for 2 more minutes, then remove from heat.
4. Roll out the puff pastry on a baking sheet and prick with a fork.
5. Spread the caramelized onions over the puff pastry, leaving a small border around the edges.
6. Sprinkle crumbled goat cheese and thyme leaves over the onions.
7. Bake in the preheated oven for 20-25 minutes, until the pastry is golden and puffed.
8. Season with salt and pepper to taste and serve warm.

Roasted Chestnut Soup

Ingredients:

- 1 lb chestnuts, peeled
- 1 onion, chopped
- 2 cloves garlic, minced
- 2 cups vegetable broth
- 1/2 cup heavy cream
- 2 tbsp butter
- Salt and pepper, to taste
- Fresh thyme for garnish

Instructions:

1. Preheat the oven to 375°F (190°C).
2. Roast the chestnuts on a baking sheet for about 15-20 minutes, then peel.
3. In a large pot, melt butter over medium heat and sauté the chopped onion and garlic until soft, about 5 minutes.
4. Add the roasted chestnuts and vegetable broth, and bring to a simmer.
5. Let the mixture simmer for about 15 minutes.
6. Use an immersion blender to blend the soup until smooth, then stir in the heavy cream.
7. Season with salt and pepper to taste.
8. Garnish with fresh thyme and serve hot.

Maple Glazed Brussels Sprouts

Ingredients:

- 1 lb Brussels sprouts, trimmed and halved
- 2 tbsp olive oil
- 1/4 cup maple syrup
- Salt and pepper, to taste
- 1/4 tsp red pepper flakes (optional)

Instructions:

1. Preheat the oven to 400°F (200°C).
2. Toss the Brussels sprouts with olive oil, salt, and pepper.
3. Spread them on a baking sheet in a single layer and roast for 20-25 minutes, shaking the pan halfway through.
4. In a small saucepan, heat the maple syrup over medium heat until it slightly thickens, about 5 minutes.
5. Drizzle the maple syrup over the roasted Brussels sprouts and toss to coat.
6. Serve immediately.

Apple Cider Glazed Pork

Ingredients:

- 2 pork chops
- 1 cup apple cider
- 1 tbsp Dijon mustard
- 1 tbsp apple cider vinegar
- 1 tbsp brown sugar
- 1 tbsp olive oil
- Salt and pepper, to taste

Instructions:

1. Season the pork chops with salt and pepper.
2. In a skillet, heat olive oil over medium-high heat. Add the pork chops and cook for 3-4 minutes on each side until browned.
3. Remove the pork chops and set them aside.
4. In the same skillet, add the apple cider, Dijon mustard, apple cider vinegar, and brown sugar. Bring to a simmer.
5. Return the pork chops to the skillet, and cook for an additional 6-8 minutes, until the pork is cooked through and the glaze thickens.
6. Serve the pork chops with the apple cider glaze.

Roasted Root Vegetables

Ingredients:

- 2 carrots, peeled and sliced
- 2 parsnips, peeled and sliced
- 1 sweet potato, peeled and cubed
- 1 red onion, quartered
- 2 tbsp olive oil
- 1 tbsp fresh rosemary, chopped
- Salt and pepper, to taste

Instructions:

1. Preheat the oven to 400°F (200°C).
2. In a large bowl, toss the vegetables with olive oil, rosemary, salt, and pepper.
3. Spread the vegetables on a baking sheet in a single layer.
4. Roast for 25-30 minutes, turning halfway through, until the vegetables are tender and golden brown.
5. Serve hot.

Mushroom Risotto with Truffle Oil

Ingredients:

- 1 cup Arborio rice
- 2 cups chicken or vegetable broth
- 1/2 cup dry white wine
- 2 tbsp butter
- 1 small onion, finely chopped
- 2 cups mushrooms, sliced
- 1/4 cup Parmesan cheese, grated
- 1 tbsp truffle oil
- Salt and pepper, to taste

Instructions:

1. In a saucepan, heat the broth over low heat.
2. In a large pan, melt the butter over medium heat. Add the onion and cook until softened, about 5 minutes.
3. Add the mushrooms and cook until browned.
4. Stir in the rice and cook for 2 minutes until lightly toasted.
5. Pour in the white wine and cook, stirring, until the wine has mostly absorbed.
6. Add the broth, one ladle at a time, stirring constantly, until the rice is tender and creamy (about 18-20 minutes).
7. Stir in the Parmesan cheese and truffle oil, then season with salt and pepper.
8. Serve immediately.

Seared Duck Breast with Fig Sauce

Ingredients:

- 2 duck breasts
- Salt and pepper, to taste
- 1/2 cup red wine
- 1/4 cup fig jam
- 1 tbsp balsamic vinegar
- 1 tbsp butter

Instructions:

1. Score the skin of the duck breasts in a crosshatch pattern and season with salt and pepper.
2. Heat a skillet over medium-high heat and sear the duck breasts, skin-side down, for about 6-7 minutes, until the skin is golden and crispy.
3. Flip the duck breasts and cook for an additional 4-5 minutes for medium-rare.
4. Remove the duck from the pan and set aside.
5. In the same pan, add the red wine, fig jam, and balsamic vinegar. Bring to a simmer and cook until the sauce has thickened, about 5 minutes.
6. Stir in the butter until smooth.
7. Slice the duck breast and serve with the fig sauce.

Chestnut and Cranberry Stuffing

Ingredients:

- 1 lb fresh chestnuts, peeled and chopped
- 1/2 cup dried cranberries
- 1 loaf of bread (preferably French or sourdough), cubed
- 1 onion, chopped
- 2 celery stalks, chopped
- 2 cloves garlic, minced
- 1/4 cup fresh parsley, chopped
- 1/4 cup fresh thyme leaves
- 2 cups vegetable or chicken broth
- 1/4 cup unsalted butter
- Salt and pepper, to taste

Instructions:

1. Preheat the oven to 350°F (175°C).
2. In a large skillet, melt the butter over medium heat. Add the onion, celery, and garlic, and cook until softened, about 5 minutes.
3. Add the chopped chestnuts, dried cranberries, parsley, and thyme, and cook for another 5 minutes.
4. In a large bowl, combine the cubed bread, chestnut mixture, and broth. Stir well, making sure the bread is moistened.
5. Season with salt and pepper to taste.
6. Transfer the mixture to a greased baking dish and cover with foil. Bake for 30 minutes, then uncover and bake for another 10-15 minutes to brown the top.

7. Serve warm.

Butternut Squash and Sage Risotto

Ingredients:

- 1 small butternut squash, peeled, seeded, and cubed
- 1 1/2 cups Arborio rice
- 1 small onion, chopped
- 2 cloves garlic, minced
- 4 cups vegetable broth, kept warm
- 1/2 cup white wine
- 2 tbsp olive oil
- 1/4 cup fresh sage leaves, chopped
- 1/2 cup Parmesan cheese, grated
- Salt and pepper, to taste

Instructions:

1. In a large pot, heat olive oil over medium heat. Add the onion and garlic, and cook until softened, about 5 minutes.
2. Add the butternut squash cubes, season with salt and pepper, and cook until slightly softened, about 8-10 minutes.
3. Add the Arborio rice and stir to coat the rice in oil. Cook for 2 minutes.
4. Pour in the white wine and cook until mostly absorbed.
5. Begin adding the warm vegetable broth one ladle at a time, stirring constantly, until the liquid is absorbed and the rice is cooked, about 20-25 minutes.
6. Stir in the Parmesan cheese and fresh sage.
7. Serve hot, garnished with extra sage if desired.

Grilled Lamb Chops with Mint Pesto

Ingredients:

- 8 lamb chops
- 1 tbsp olive oil
- Salt and pepper, to taste
- 1 cup fresh mint leaves
- 1/4 cup fresh parsley leaves
- 1/4 cup pine nuts
- 1/4 cup Parmesan cheese, grated
- 1/2 cup olive oil
- 1 tbsp lemon juice

Instructions:

1. Preheat the grill to medium-high heat.
2. Season the lamb chops with olive oil, salt, and pepper.
3. Grill the lamb chops for 3-4 minutes per side for medium-rare, or longer if desired.
4. While the lamb chops are grilling, prepare the mint pesto: Combine the mint, parsley, pine nuts, Parmesan, olive oil, and lemon juice in a food processor. Pulse until smooth.
5. Serve the grilled lamb chops with a drizzle of mint pesto on top.

Pear and Blue Cheese Salad

Ingredients:

- 2 pears, sliced
- 4 cups mixed greens (arugula, spinach, etc.)
- 1/4 cup crumbled blue cheese
- 1/4 cup toasted walnuts
- 1 tbsp olive oil
- 1 tbsp balsamic vinegar
- Salt and pepper, to taste

Instructions:

1. In a large bowl, toss the mixed greens with olive oil and balsamic vinegar.
2. Add the pear slices, blue cheese, and toasted walnuts.
3. Season with salt and pepper.
4. Serve immediately.

Beef and Pumpkin Chili

Ingredients:

- 1 lb ground beef
- 1 small pumpkin, peeled, seeded, and cubed
- 1 onion, chopped
- 2 cloves garlic, minced
- 1 can diced tomatoes
- 2 cups beef broth
- 1 tbsp chili powder
- 1 tsp ground cumin
- 1 tsp smoked paprika
- 1/2 tsp cinnamon
- Salt and pepper, to taste

Instructions:

1. In a large pot, cook the ground beef over medium heat until browned. Drain any excess fat.
2. Add the onion and garlic to the pot, and cook until softened, about 5 minutes.
3. Add the pumpkin cubes, diced tomatoes, beef broth, chili powder, cumin, paprika, and cinnamon.
4. Bring to a simmer and cook for 30-40 minutes, until the pumpkin is tender and the chili thickens.
5. Season with salt and pepper to taste.
6. Serve hot with optional toppings such as sour cream, cheese, or cilantro.

Roasted Pumpkin Seeds

Ingredients:

- 1 pumpkin, seeds removed
- 1 tbsp olive oil
- 1 tsp salt
- 1/2 tsp ground paprika (optional)
- 1/2 tsp ground cumin (optional)

Instructions:

1. Preheat the oven to 350°F (175°C).
2. Clean the pumpkin seeds by removing any pulp and rinsing them under cold water.
3. Pat the seeds dry with a towel.
4. Toss the seeds with olive oil, salt, and any desired spices.
5. Spread the seeds in a single layer on a baking sheet.
6. Roast for 15-20 minutes, stirring halfway through, until golden and crispy.
7. Let cool before serving.

Spicy Carrot and Ginger Soup

Ingredients:

- 1 lb carrots, peeled and chopped
- 1 onion, chopped
- 2 cloves garlic, minced
- 1-inch piece of ginger, grated
- 4 cups vegetable broth
- 1 tbsp olive oil
- 1/4 tsp red pepper flakes
- Salt and pepper, to taste

Instructions:

1. In a large pot, heat olive oil over medium heat. Add the onion, garlic, and ginger, and cook until softened, about 5 minutes.
2. Add the chopped carrots and cook for another 5 minutes.
3. Pour in the vegetable broth and bring to a boil.
4. Reduce the heat and simmer until the carrots are tender, about 20 minutes.
5. Use an immersion blender or regular blender to puree the soup until smooth.
6. Season with salt, pepper, and red pepper flakes for extra heat.
7. Serve hot.

Roasted Beet Salad with Goat Cheese

Ingredients:

- 4 medium beets, peeled and roasted
- 4 cups mixed greens
- 1/4 cup goat cheese, crumbled
- 1/4 cup toasted walnuts
- 2 tbsp olive oil
- 1 tbsp balsamic vinegar
- Salt and pepper, to taste

Instructions:

1. Preheat the oven to 400°F (200°C).
2. Wrap the beets in foil and roast for 40-45 minutes, until tender. Let cool, then peel and slice.
3. In a large bowl, toss the mixed greens with olive oil and balsamic vinegar.
4. Add the roasted beets, goat cheese, and toasted walnuts.
5. Season with salt and pepper, and serve immediately.

Braised Short Ribs with Root Vegetables

Ingredients:

- 4 beef short ribs
- 2 tbsp olive oil
- 1 onion, chopped
- 2 carrots, chopped
- 2 parsnips, chopped
- 2 cloves garlic, minced
- 2 cups red wine
- 3 cups beef broth
- 1 tbsp fresh thyme leaves
- Salt and pepper, to taste

Instructions:

1. Preheat the oven to 350°F (175°C).
2. In a large Dutch oven, heat olive oil over medium-high heat. Season the short ribs with salt and pepper, and sear them on all sides until browned, about 5 minutes per side.
3. Remove the short ribs and set them aside.
4. Add the onion, carrots, parsnips, and garlic to the pot, and cook for 5 minutes until softened.
5. Add the red wine, scraping up any browned bits from the bottom of the pot.
6. Return the short ribs to the pot, add the beef broth and thyme, and bring to a simmer.
7. Cover the pot and transfer to the oven. Braise for 2-2.5 hours, until the meat is tender.
8. Serve the short ribs with the braised vegetables.

Cider-Braised Chicken

Ingredients:

- 4 bone-in, skin-on chicken thighs
- 2 tbsp olive oil
- 1 onion, chopped
- 2 cloves garlic, minced
- 1 cup apple cider
- 2 tbsp Dijon mustard
- 1 tbsp fresh thyme leaves
- Salt and pepper, to taste

Instructions:

1. In a large skillet, heat olive oil over medium-high heat. Season the chicken thighs with salt and pepper, and sear them on both sides until golden brown, about 5 minutes per side.
2. Remove the chicken and set aside.
3. Add the onion and garlic to the skillet and cook for 5 minutes until softened.
4. Stir in the apple cider, Dijon mustard, and thyme, and bring to a simmer.
5. Return the chicken to the skillet, skin-side up, and cover.
6. Cook on low for 25-30 minutes, until the chicken is fully cooked.
7. Serve with the cider sauce and garnish with extra thyme.

Pumpkin and Ricotta Gnocchi

Ingredients:

- 1 cup pumpkin puree
- 1 cup ricotta cheese
- 1 1/2 cups all-purpose flour (plus extra for dusting)
- 1 egg
- 1/2 tsp ground nutmeg
- Salt and pepper, to taste
- 1/4 cup unsalted butter
- Fresh sage leaves, for garnish
- Parmesan cheese, grated (optional)

Instructions:

1. In a large bowl, combine the pumpkin puree, ricotta, egg, nutmeg, salt, and pepper. Gradually add the flour, mixing until a dough forms.
2. Transfer the dough to a floured surface and knead gently until smooth, about 2-3 minutes.
3. Divide the dough into 4 equal parts. Roll each part into a long rope about 1/2 inch thick. Cut into 1-inch pieces to form gnocchi.
4. Use a fork to gently press each piece to create ridges.
5. Bring a large pot of salted water to a boil. Drop the gnocchi in batches into the water and cook until they float to the surface, about 2-3 minutes. Remove with a slotted spoon.
6. In a large skillet, melt the butter over medium heat. Add the sage leaves and cook until crispy, about 2 minutes.
7. Toss the cooked gnocchi in the sage butter. Serve immediately with grated Parmesan if desired.

Roasted Apple and Squash Soup

Ingredients:

- 1 small butternut squash, peeled and cubed
- 2 apples, peeled, cored, and chopped
- 1 onion, chopped
- 2 cloves garlic, minced
- 4 cups vegetable or chicken broth
- 1 tsp ground cinnamon
- 1/2 tsp ground ginger
- Salt and pepper, to taste
- 2 tbsp olive oil
- 1/4 cup heavy cream (optional)

Instructions:

1. Preheat the oven to 400°F (200°C).
2. On a baking sheet, toss the cubed squash and apple pieces with olive oil, cinnamon, ginger, salt, and pepper. Roast for 25-30 minutes until tender and slightly caramelized.
3. In a large pot, sauté the onion and garlic in olive oil over medium heat until softened, about 5 minutes.
4. Add the roasted squash and apples to the pot, followed by the broth. Bring to a simmer and cook for 10 minutes.
5. Use an immersion blender to puree the soup until smooth (or transfer to a blender in batches).
6. Stir in heavy cream if using, and adjust seasoning with salt and pepper.
7. Serve warm, garnished with a drizzle of cream or roasted seeds if desired.

Maple-Glazed Carrots

Ingredients:

- 1 lb carrots, peeled and sliced
- 2 tbsp unsalted butter
- 3 tbsp maple syrup
- 1 tbsp fresh thyme leaves
- Salt and pepper, to taste

Instructions:

1. In a large skillet, melt the butter over medium heat.
2. Add the sliced carrots and sauté for 5-7 minutes until slightly tender.
3. Pour in the maple syrup, and season with salt and pepper. Cook for another 5-7 minutes, stirring occasionally, until the carrots are tender and glazed.
4. Garnish with fresh thyme leaves and serve immediately.

Autumn Harvest Salad

Ingredients:

- 4 cups mixed greens (arugula, spinach, or kale)
- 1 apple, thinly sliced
- 1/2 cup roasted butternut squash cubes
- 1/4 cup pomegranate seeds
- 1/4 cup candied pecans
- 1/4 cup crumbled feta or goat cheese
- 2 tbsp olive oil
- 1 tbsp apple cider vinegar
- 1 tsp honey
- Salt and pepper, to taste

Instructions:

1. In a large bowl, combine the mixed greens, apple slices, roasted squash, pomegranate seeds, pecans, and cheese.
2. In a small bowl, whisk together the olive oil, apple cider vinegar, honey, salt, and pepper.
3. Drizzle the dressing over the salad and toss gently to combine.
4. Serve immediately as a side dish or light main course.

Butternut Squash and Sage Flatbread

Ingredients:

- 1 small butternut squash, peeled, cubed, and roasted
- 1 package pizza dough (store-bought or homemade)
- 1/4 cup olive oil
- 1/4 cup fresh sage leaves
- 1/4 tsp ground cinnamon
- Salt and pepper, to taste
- 1/2 cup ricotta cheese (optional)
- 1/4 cup grated Parmesan cheese

Instructions:

1. Preheat the oven to 450°F (230°C).
2. Roll out the pizza dough on a floured surface to your desired thickness. Place on a baking sheet.
3. In a small bowl, toss the roasted butternut squash with olive oil, cinnamon, salt, and pepper. Spread the squash evenly over the flatbread dough.
4. Sprinkle the sage leaves and Parmesan cheese on top.
5. Bake for 12-15 minutes, or until the edges of the flatbread are golden and crispy.
6. If using, top with ricotta cheese before serving.

Pecan-Crusted Salmon

Ingredients:

- 4 salmon fillets
- 1/2 cup pecans, chopped
- 1/4 cup panko breadcrumbs
- 2 tbsp Dijon mustard
- 1 tbsp maple syrup
- 1 tbsp olive oil
- Salt and pepper, to taste

Instructions:

1. Preheat the oven to 375°F (190°C).
2. In a small bowl, mix together the chopped pecans, panko breadcrumbs, salt, and pepper.
3. In another small bowl, whisk together the Dijon mustard, maple syrup, and olive oil.
4. Place the salmon fillets on a baking sheet lined with parchment paper. Brush the top of each fillet with the mustard-syrup mixture.
5. Press the pecan breadcrumb mixture onto the top of each fillet.
6. Bake for 12-15 minutes, or until the salmon is cooked through and the crust is golden.
7. Serve immediately.

Braised Lamb Shanks with Root Vegetables

Ingredients:

- 4 lamb shanks
- 2 tbsp olive oil
- 1 onion, chopped
- 2 carrots, chopped
- 2 parsnips, chopped
- 2 garlic cloves, minced
- 2 cups red wine
- 3 cups beef broth
- 2 sprigs rosemary
- 2 sprigs thyme
- Salt and pepper, to taste

Instructions:

1. Preheat the oven to 350°F (175°C).
2. In a large Dutch oven, heat olive oil over medium-high heat. Season the lamb shanks with salt and pepper, then sear them on all sides until browned, about 4 minutes per side.
3. Remove the lamb shanks and set aside.
4. Add the onion, carrots, parsnips, and garlic to the pot, and cook for 5 minutes until softened.
5. Pour in the red wine and simmer for 5 minutes, scraping up any browned bits.
6. Return the lamb shanks to the pot, and add the beef broth, rosemary, and thyme. Bring to a simmer.

7. Cover the pot and transfer to the oven. Braise for 2-2.5 hours, until the lamb is tender and falling off the bone.

8. Serve with the braised vegetables.

Sweet Potato and Kale Salad

Ingredients:

- 2 medium sweet potatoes, peeled and cubed
- 2 tbsp olive oil
- Salt and pepper, to taste
- 4 cups kale, stems removed and chopped
- 1/4 cup toasted sunflower seeds
- 1/4 cup dried cranberries
- 2 tbsp olive oil (for dressing)
- 1 tbsp apple cider vinegar
- 1 tsp Dijon mustard

Instructions:

1. Preheat the oven to 400°F (200°C).
2. Toss the sweet potato cubes with olive oil, salt, and pepper. Spread in a single layer on a baking sheet and roast for 25-30 minutes, until tender and lightly caramelized.
3. In a large bowl, massage the kale with olive oil and a pinch of salt for 2-3 minutes until softened.
4. Add the roasted sweet potatoes, sunflower seeds, and cranberries to the kale.
5. In a small bowl, whisk together the olive oil, vinegar, and Dijon mustard for the dressing.
6. Drizzle the dressing over the salad and toss to combine.
7. Serve immediately.

Spiced Pear Cake

Ingredients:

- 2 pears, peeled, cored, and chopped
- 1 1/2 cups all-purpose flour
- 1 tsp baking powder
- 1/2 tsp ground cinnamon
- 1/4 tsp ground ginger
- 1/4 tsp ground cloves
- 1/2 cup unsalted butter, softened
- 1 cup sugar
- 2 eggs
- 1/2 cup milk
- 1 tsp vanilla extract
- Pinch of salt

Instructions:

1. Preheat the oven to 350°F (175°C). Grease and flour a 9-inch cake pan.
2. In a bowl, whisk together the flour, baking powder, cinnamon, ginger, cloves, and salt.
3. In a separate large bowl, cream together the butter and sugar until light and fluffy.
4. Add the eggs one at a time, beating well after each addition.
5. Add the dry ingredients to the wet ingredients in alternating batches with the milk, starting and ending with the dry ingredients.
6. Fold in the chopped pears.

7. Pour the batter into the prepared cake pan and smooth the top.

8. Bake for 35-40 minutes, or until a toothpick inserted into the center comes out clean.

9. Let the cake cool in the pan for 10 minutes before transferring to a wire rack to cool completely.

10. Serve as is or with a dollop of whipped cream or ice cream.

Roasted Brussels Sprouts with Pancetta

Ingredients:

- 1 lb Brussels sprouts, trimmed and halved
- 4 oz pancetta, diced
- 2 tbsp olive oil
- 2 cloves garlic, minced
- Salt and pepper, to taste
- 1/4 cup grated Parmesan cheese (optional)

Instructions:

1. Preheat the oven to 400°F (200°C).
2. In a large bowl, toss the Brussels sprouts with olive oil, garlic, salt, and pepper.
3. Arrange the Brussels sprouts on a baking sheet in a single layer.
4. Scatter the diced pancetta over the sprouts.
5. Roast for 20-25 minutes, tossing halfway through, until the Brussels sprouts are crispy and golden and the pancetta is crisp.
6. If desired, sprinkle with Parmesan cheese before serving.

Cranberry and Orange Glazed Turkey

Ingredients:

- 1 whole turkey (10-12 lbs)
- 1 cup fresh cranberries
- 1/2 cup orange juice
- 1/4 cup honey
- 1/4 cup butter, melted
- 1 tsp ground cinnamon
- Salt and pepper, to taste
- 2 tbsp olive oil

Instructions:

1. Preheat the oven to 325°F (165°C).
2. Rub the turkey with olive oil, salt, and pepper.
3. Place the turkey in a roasting pan, breast side up, and roast according to the turkey's weight (typically about 15 minutes per pound).
4. While the turkey roasts, make the cranberry and orange glaze: In a saucepan, combine the cranberries, orange juice, honey, butter, and cinnamon. Bring to a simmer over medium heat. Stir occasionally and cook for 10-15 minutes until the cranberries burst and the sauce thickens.
5. During the last 30 minutes of roasting, brush the turkey with the cranberry-orange glaze every 10 minutes.
6. Once the turkey is cooked through, remove it from the oven and let it rest for 15-20 minutes before carving. Serve with extra glaze on the side.

Roasted Pumpkin with Parmesan

Ingredients:

- 1 medium pumpkin, peeled and cubed
- 2 tbsp olive oil
- Salt and pepper, to taste
- 1/4 cup grated Parmesan cheese
- 1/2 tsp ground nutmeg
- Fresh thyme leaves, for garnish

Instructions:

1. Preheat the oven to 375°F (190°C).
2. Toss the pumpkin cubes with olive oil, salt, pepper, and nutmeg.
3. Spread the pumpkin in a single layer on a baking sheet.
4. Roast for 25-30 minutes, until tender and slightly golden.
5. Sprinkle with Parmesan cheese during the last 5 minutes of roasting.
6. Garnish with fresh thyme before serving.

Herb-Crusted Pork Tenderloin

Ingredients:

- 2 pork tenderloins (about 1 lb each)
- 2 tbsp olive oil
- 2 tbsp fresh rosemary, chopped
- 1 tbsp fresh thyme, chopped
- 2 cloves garlic, minced
- 1 tbsp Dijon mustard
- Salt and pepper, to taste

Instructions:

1. Preheat the oven to 400°F (200°C).
2. In a small bowl, combine the rosemary, thyme, garlic, mustard, olive oil, salt, and pepper.
3. Rub the herb mixture all over the pork tenderloins.
4. Heat a skillet over medium-high heat and sear the tenderloins on all sides until browned, about 3-4 minutes per side.
5. Transfer the pork to a baking sheet and roast for 20-25 minutes, until the internal temperature reaches 145°F (63°C).
6. Let the pork rest for 5 minutes before slicing and serving.

Spicy Apple Chutney

Ingredients:

- 4 apples, peeled, cored, and chopped
- 1/2 onion, chopped
- 1/4 cup brown sugar
- 1/4 cup apple cider vinegar
- 1/4 cup raisins
- 1 tbsp grated fresh ginger
- 1/2 tsp ground cinnamon
- 1/4 tsp ground cloves
- 1/2 tsp red pepper flakes (or more for extra heat)
- Salt, to taste

Instructions:

1. In a large saucepan, combine all ingredients.
2. Bring to a simmer over medium heat, stirring occasionally.
3. Cook for 30-40 minutes, until the apples have softened and the chutney has thickened.
4. Remove from heat and let it cool before serving.
5. Store in the fridge for up to a week.

Baked Acorn Squash with Quinoa

Ingredients:

- 2 acorn squashes, halved and seeded
- 1 cup cooked quinoa
- 1/4 cup dried cranberries
- 1/4 cup chopped pecans
- 2 tbsp maple syrup
- 1 tbsp olive oil
- Salt and pepper, to taste

Instructions:

1. Preheat the oven to 375°F (190°C).
2. Place the squash halves on a baking sheet, drizzle with olive oil, and season with salt and pepper.
3. Roast for 25-30 minutes, until the squash is tender.
4. In a bowl, combine the cooked quinoa, cranberries, pecans, and maple syrup.
5. Once the squash is done, fill the center of each half with the quinoa mixture.
6. Return the squash to the oven and bake for another 10 minutes.
7. Serve warm.

Pear and Arugula Salad with Walnuts

Ingredients:

- 4 cups arugula
- 2 pears, sliced
- 1/4 cup walnuts, toasted
- 1/4 cup crumbled blue cheese or goat cheese
- 2 tbsp olive oil
- 1 tbsp balsamic vinegar
- 1 tsp honey
- Salt and pepper, to taste

Instructions:

1. In a large bowl, toss the arugula, pear slices, walnuts, and cheese.
2. In a small bowl, whisk together the olive oil, balsamic vinegar, honey, salt, and pepper.
3. Drizzle the dressing over the salad and toss gently.
4. Serve immediately.

Autumn Vegetable Gratin

Ingredients:

- 2 cups thinly sliced potatoes
- 1 cup thinly sliced sweet potatoes
- 1 cup thinly sliced butternut squash
- 1 cup heavy cream
- 1 cup shredded Gruyère cheese
- 1/2 tsp ground nutmeg
- Salt and pepper, to taste

Instructions:

1. Preheat the oven to 375°F (190°C).
2. In a greased baking dish, layer the sliced potatoes, sweet potatoes, and squash.
3. In a small saucepan, heat the cream over medium heat. Stir in the nutmeg, salt, and pepper.
4. Pour the cream mixture over the vegetables.
5. Sprinkle the cheese evenly on top.
6. Cover with foil and bake for 30 minutes.
7. Remove the foil and bake for an additional 15-20 minutes, until the top is golden and bubbly.
8. Let it cool for a few minutes before serving.

Chestnut-Stuffed Chicken

Ingredients:

- 4 boneless, skinless chicken breasts
- 1 cup cooked chestnuts, chopped
- 1/2 cup breadcrumbs
- 1/4 cup fresh parsley, chopped
- 1/4 cup grated Parmesan cheese
- 1 tbsp olive oil
- Salt and pepper, to taste

Instructions:

1. Preheat the oven to 375°F (190°C).
2. In a bowl, combine the chestnuts, breadcrumbs, parsley, Parmesan, olive oil, salt, and pepper.
3. Cut a pocket into the side of each chicken breast and stuff with the chestnut mixture.
4. Secure with toothpicks if necessary.
5. Heat olive oil in a skillet over medium-high heat. Sear the chicken breasts for 3-4 minutes per side until golden brown.
6. Transfer the chicken to the oven and bake for 20-25 minutes, or until the internal temperature reaches 165°F (74°C).
7. Remove the toothpicks and serve.

Roasted Sweet Potato with Cinnamon

Ingredients:

- 2 large sweet potatoes, peeled and cubed
- 2 tbsp olive oil
- 1 tsp ground cinnamon
- 1/4 tsp ground nutmeg
- Salt and pepper, to taste

Instructions:

1. Preheat the oven to 400°F (200°C).
2. Toss the sweet potato cubes with olive oil, cinnamon, nutmeg, salt, and pepper.
3. Spread the cubes in a single layer on a baking sheet.
4. Roast for 25-30 minutes, flipping halfway through, until the sweet potatoes are tender and golden.
5. Serve warm.

Apple Crisp

Ingredients:

- 6 apples, peeled, cored, and sliced
- 1 cup rolled oats
- 1/2 cup brown sugar
- 1/2 cup all-purpose flour
- 1/4 cup unsalted butter, softened
- 1/2 tsp ground cinnamon
- 1/4 tsp ground nutmeg
- Pinch of salt

Instructions:

1. Preheat the oven to 350°F (175°C).
2. In a large bowl, combine the sliced apples, cinnamon, nutmeg, and a pinch of salt. Toss to coat the apples evenly.
3. Transfer the apple mixture to a greased 9x13 baking dish.
4. In a separate bowl, mix the oats, brown sugar, flour, and butter until it forms a crumbly mixture.
5. Sprinkle the oat mixture evenly over the apples.
6. Bake for 45-50 minutes, until the top is golden and the apples are tender.
7. Serve warm with vanilla ice cream or whipped cream.

Cinnamon Baked Pears

Ingredients:

- 4 pears, halved and cored
- 1/4 cup honey
- 1 tsp ground cinnamon
- 1/4 tsp ground nutmeg
- 1 tbsp butter
- 1/4 cup chopped pecans (optional)

Instructions:

1. Preheat the oven to 350°F (175°C).
2. Place the pear halves in a baking dish, cut side up.
3. Drizzle with honey and sprinkle with cinnamon, nutmeg, and chopped pecans (if using).
4. Place a small piece of butter on each pear half.
5. Cover with foil and bake for 30-35 minutes, until the pears are tender.
6. Serve warm, optionally with a dollop of whipped cream or a scoop of ice cream.

Stuffed Acorn Squash

Ingredients:

- 2 acorn squashes, halved and seeded
- 1 cup cooked quinoa
- 1/4 cup dried cranberries
- 1/4 cup chopped walnuts
- 2 tbsp maple syrup
- Salt and pepper, to taste
- 2 tbsp olive oil

Instructions:

1. Preheat the oven to 375°F (190°C).
2. Drizzle the squash halves with olive oil, salt, and pepper.
3. Place them on a baking sheet, cut side down, and roast for 30-40 minutes, until tender.
4. In a bowl, combine the cooked quinoa, cranberries, walnuts, and maple syrup.
5. Once the squash is roasted, fill the centers with the quinoa mixture.
6. Return to the oven for 10 minutes to warm through.
7. Serve warm.

Wild Mushroom and Spinach Frittata

Ingredients:

- 1 tbsp olive oil
- 1/2 cup wild mushrooms, sliced
- 1/2 cup fresh spinach, chopped
- 6 large eggs
- 1/4 cup milk
- 1/2 cup shredded mozzarella cheese
- Salt and pepper, to taste

Instructions:

1. Preheat the oven to 350°F (175°C).
2. In an oven-safe skillet, heat olive oil over medium heat. Add the mushrooms and cook for 5-7 minutes until soft.
3. Add the spinach and cook for another 1-2 minutes, until wilted.
4. In a bowl, whisk together the eggs, milk, salt, and pepper. Pour the egg mixture over the mushrooms and spinach.
5. Sprinkle the shredded mozzarella cheese on top.
6. Bake in the oven for 15-20 minutes, until the eggs are set and the top is golden.
7. Slice and serve warm.

Caramelized Apple and Onion Tart

Ingredients:

- 1 sheet puff pastry
- 2 apples, thinly sliced
- 1 large onion, thinly sliced
- 2 tbsp butter
- 1 tbsp olive oil
- 1 tbsp brown sugar
- 1 tsp fresh thyme leaves
- Salt and pepper, to taste
- 1/4 cup crumbled goat cheese or brie (optional)

Instructions:

1. Preheat the oven to 400°F (200°C).
2. In a skillet, melt the butter and olive oil over medium heat. Add the onions and cook for 15-20 minutes, stirring occasionally, until caramelized.
3. Add the apples, brown sugar, thyme, salt, and pepper. Cook for 5-7 minutes until the apples are tender and slightly caramelized.
4. Roll out the puff pastry on a baking sheet lined with parchment paper.
5. Spread the caramelized apple and onion mixture evenly over the pastry.
6. If desired, sprinkle with goat cheese or brie.
7. Bake for 20-25 minutes, until the pastry is golden and crisp.
8. Serve warm.

Pumpkin Spice Cheesecake

Ingredients:

- 1 1/2 cups graham cracker crumbs
- 1/4 cup sugar
- 1/4 cup melted butter
- 3 cups cream cheese, softened
- 1 cup pumpkin puree
- 1/2 cup sugar
- 2 large eggs
- 1 tsp vanilla extract
- 1 tsp ground cinnamon
- 1/2 tsp ground ginger
- 1/4 tsp ground nutmeg
- 1/4 tsp ground cloves
- 1/4 tsp salt

Instructions:

1. Preheat the oven to 325°F (165°C).
2. In a bowl, mix the graham cracker crumbs, sugar, and melted butter. Press the mixture into the bottom of a 9-inch springform pan to form the crust.
3. Bake for 10 minutes, then remove from the oven and set aside.
4. In a large bowl, beat the cream cheese until smooth. Add the pumpkin, sugar, eggs, vanilla, cinnamon, ginger, nutmeg, cloves, and salt. Mix until smooth.
5. Pour the mixture over the crust in the springform pan.

6. Bake for 50-60 minutes, until the center is set. Let cool completely before refrigerating for at least 4 hours.

7. Serve chilled, optionally topped with whipped cream.

Grilled Squash and Zucchini Salad

Ingredients:

- 1 zucchini, sliced
- 1 yellow squash, sliced
- 1 tbsp olive oil
- Salt and pepper, to taste
- 1/4 cup crumbled feta cheese
- 1/4 cup toasted pine nuts
- 2 tbsp fresh basil, chopped
- 1 tbsp balsamic vinegar

Instructions:

1. Preheat the grill to medium heat.
2. Toss the zucchini and squash slices with olive oil, salt, and pepper.
3. Grill the vegetables for 3-4 minutes per side, until tender and slightly charred.
4. Arrange the grilled vegetables on a platter.
5. Sprinkle with feta cheese, pine nuts, and fresh basil.
6. Drizzle with balsamic vinegar and serve warm or at room temperature.

Maple Roasted Sweet Potatoes

Ingredients:

- 4 medium sweet potatoes, peeled and cubed
- 2 tbsp olive oil
- 2 tbsp maple syrup
- 1/2 tsp ground cinnamon
- Salt and pepper, to taste

Instructions:

1. Preheat the oven to 375°F (190°C).
2. Toss the sweet potato cubes with olive oil, maple syrup, cinnamon, salt, and pepper.
3. Spread the cubes in a single layer on a baking sheet.
4. Roast for 25-30 minutes, tossing halfway through, until the sweet potatoes are tender and caramelized.
5. Serve warm.

Baked Apple with Cinnamon and Nuts

Ingredients:

- 4 apples, cored
- 1/4 cup chopped walnuts or pecans
- 2 tbsp honey
- 1 tsp ground cinnamon
- 1/4 tsp ground nutmeg
- 1/4 cup raisins (optional)

Instructions:

1. Preheat the oven to 350°F (175°C).
2. Place the apples in a baking dish.
3. In a small bowl, mix the chopped nuts, honey, cinnamon, nutmeg, and raisins (if using).
4. Stuff the apples with the nut mixture.
5. Bake for 25-30 minutes, until the apples are tender.
6. Serve warm with a drizzle of honey or a scoop of ice cream.

Apple and Pork Sausage Stuffing

Ingredients:

- 1 lb pork sausage
- 1/2 cup onion, chopped
- 1/2 cup celery, chopped
- 2 apples, peeled, cored, and chopped
- 6 cups cubed stale bread
- 1/4 cup chicken broth
- 1 tsp ground sage
- Salt and pepper, to taste

Instructions:

1. Preheat the oven to 350°F (175°C).
2. In a large skillet, cook the sausage until browned. Remove from the skillet and set aside.
3. In the same skillet, sauté the onion, celery, and apples until soft.
4. Add the sausage back into the skillet, then stir in the cubed bread, chicken broth, sage, salt, and pepper.
5. Transfer to a baking dish and cover with foil.
6. Bake for 30-35 minutes, until golden brown.

Carrot and Sweet Potato Soup

Ingredients:

- 2 tbsp olive oil
- 1 onion, chopped
- 2 garlic cloves, minced
- 3 carrots, peeled and chopped
- 2 medium sweet potatoes, peeled and chopped
- 4 cups vegetable broth
- 1/2 tsp ground cumin
- Salt and pepper, to taste

Instructions:

1. Heat olive oil in a large pot over medium heat.
2. Add the onion and garlic and sauté until softened.
3. Add the carrots, sweet potatoes, vegetable broth, cumin, salt, and pepper.
4. Bring to a boil, then reduce heat and simmer for 25-30 minutes, until the vegetables are tender.
5. Blend the soup until smooth using an immersion blender or regular blender.
6. Serve warm.

Spiced Pumpkin Cake with Cream Cheese Frosting

Ingredients:
For the cake:

- 1 1/2 cups all-purpose flour
- 1 tsp baking soda
- 1/2 tsp ground cinnamon
- 1/4 tsp ground nutmeg
- 1/4 tsp ground cloves
- 1/4 tsp ground ginger
- 1/2 tsp salt
- 1/2 cup vegetable oil
- 1 cup granulated sugar
- 2 large eggs
- 1 cup pumpkin puree

For the frosting:

- 8 oz cream cheese, softened
- 1/4 cup unsalted butter, softened
- 1 1/2 cups powdered sugar
- 1 tsp vanilla extract

Instructions:

1. Preheat the oven to 350°F (175°C).
2. In a bowl, whisk together the flour, baking soda, spices, and salt.

3. In another bowl, whisk together the oil, sugar, eggs, and pumpkin puree.

4. Add the dry ingredients to the wet ingredients and mix until combined.

5. Pour the batter into a greased 9x13 baking pan and bake for 30-35 minutes.

6. While the cake is cooling, make the frosting by beating the cream cheese, butter, powdered sugar, and vanilla until smooth.

7. Frost the cooled cake and serve.